INTIMACIES
&
OTHER DEVICES

ALSO BY
KURT HEINZELMAN

POETRY
The Halfway Tree
Black Butterflies
The Names They Found There

TRANSLATION
Demarcations: A Translation of Jean Follain's Territoires (1953)

LITERARY HISTORY
The Economics of the Imagination

EDITIONS
Make It New: The Rise of Modernism
The Covarrubias Circle

INTIMACIES
&
OTHER
DEVICES

BY

KURT
HEINZELMAN

PINYON PUBLISHING

Montrose, Colorado

Cover Painting: *A Young Woman Reading*, 1875 (oil on panel),
Lucius Rossi (1846-1913) / Clark Institute, Williamstown, MA,
USA / The Bridgeman Art Library

Book and Cover Design by Susan E. Elliott

Photograph of Kurt Heinzelman by Christina S. Murrey

First Edition: September 2013

Pinyon Publishing
23847 V66 Trail, Montrose, CO 81403
www.pinyon-publishing.com

Library of Congress Control Number: 2013946776
ISBN: 978-1-936671-19-9

Acknowledgments

Some of the poems in this book were first published in other media, sometimes in different forms. I am grateful to these publications and to their editors.

"A Problem, Explaining," *Hotel Amerika*

"And Talks to His Own Self Howe'er He Pleases," *Rowboat*

"Cabbage Hauling," *Pinyon Review*

"Career Moves," *The Dirty Goat*

"Carnal Suite," *The Dirty Goat*

"Conversation, With Feeling," wall panel with portrait of Verlaine by Anders Zorn (1860-1920), exhibition of nineteenth-century French prints, Blanton Museum of Art

"Daphne: A Pindaric Ode," exhibition catalogue for *Desire*, Blanton Museum of Art

"Embouchure," *di-verse-city 2011: Austin International Poetry Festival Anthology*

"*Femme Paysage*," *Pinyon Review*

"Hang Up Please and Try Dialing Again," *The Massachusetts Review*

"Laying the Table," *The Blanton Poetry Project*, Blanton Museum of Art Exhibition

"Lust, At Your Age," *The Massachusetts Review*

"Pousse-Café," *Borderlands: Texas Poetry Review*

"Sister Noire," *Blue Mesa Review*

"Slow Dancing With Who Brung Ya," *RiverSedge*

"Texas Sleeping-Car Ballads," *The Dirty Goat*

"The Wound of Water in the Stones of the Day," *The Dirty Goat*

TO

Umi / Amu

*There does not exist a real
intimacy that is repellent.
All the spaces of intimacy
are designated by attraction.
Their being is well-being.*

—Gaston Bachelard

CONTENTS

HISTORY OF THE BALLAD

INTIMACIES: A CHORALE

FURTHER DISTURBANCES

HISTORY OF THE
BALLAD

HISTORY OF THE BALLAD

tres canciones y un corrido

i. *Canción*: "Lady, with Horsemen"

Her horse is black,
the air more sheen
than mist in which
the lady's riding,
short of a canter,
in her full-length
roseate-hued
guayabera,
four caballeros
all named Rossman
down from the North
to meet her at
the arroyo's mouth,
when out of it
come herds of cloud,
a head-wind lowing,
leaving its brand
on every flank,
and the other
horsemen up from
the South all named
Carlos galloping
hard like banditos
whom the pink tongues
of air want to
bind closer to her
than wedlock but
without any
force of arms or
force of habit—

nothing to drive
off all those mixed
feelings she rode
this far out to be
certain not to miss
or to give at least
a sweet lashing to.

ii. *Canción*: "Lady, With Wrangler"

However my hands were wont to enter
the hip pockets of your designer
jeans, they never had any design on you,
I swear, my lady, beyond the mildest
castellations of male desire.

Every giddy-up had long ago
left all my little doggies,
these saddlebags my only fruit.
No blood on the saddle,
no mud on any spur, or boot.

I have wanted, yes, to hold you,
to keep you close, so close
your own eyes would close
were I to sleep. And open, then, to
the other side of wrangling dreams.

Which is why this high noon
I have brought you this. For us
to hold. This handful of figures
cursive, like the rhinestone ones
on your jeans, parsing the intimate parts

of our being together together.

iii. *Canción*: "Lady of the Body Parlors"

Concentration
        worthy of lovers
means learning to
        learn what to ignore.
The death's head, for
        example, on her
shoulder. The rings—
        four in one ear, five
in the other.
        The stud in the nose,
tongue and navel.
        The linked nipple rings.
Now he's cupping
        in his palms the wings
fledging across
        the base of her spine,
hands spidering
        down to where her flesh
orbs into its
        own twin hemispheres,
but she keels off
        him, her rings keening
their old chanteys
        about being tied
down, and yes, wings
        are flexing, flexing
but it's more like
        wind flensing the web
from the spider
        than it is like what
he wants: to be

together flying
or to have flown,
          swans or gods, but not
left just scribal
          here, all ink and chains.

iv. *Corrido*: Boss-Lady of Want

I found you pale and compliant
I found you fisted as ropes
I found you belled and ringing
and so I said
sleep with me
sleep with any one of my sons
or sleep with all of them
for this town is yours
I said and the whole
countryside besides
we'll pluck we'll strum
in any key you wish
sing
sing or hum
it's your throat we love
also the pleats
in your blouse
the way you make them unfold
also your chaps
(we love chaps)
also spurs
the way the dogs follow
wherever you walk
the way the seashells
collect at your feet
wherever you sit
and nobody owes you
nothing honey
not even the Indians
still left in these parts
who adore you

SLOW DANCING WITH WHO BRUNG YA

It would come to pass in her mother's cellar
where they went to dance and then to neck
among the rows of vases, her dark cannings,
and potted stumps of wintering geraniums

with tendrils overhead of all things drying.
Cheek to cheek at first, then by turns turning into
half-steps, arm over arm, they reached the shelf
where some cans oozed and an open one housed

a dead wren. His were not hands that left her
open, open, or crying out in tongues, she cried,
or that is how she later felt, after what was
left was all mothering would have to show for it:

the mason jars of sacrifice, stacked far away
from where dawn thumbed the moisture off
the edge of leaves and spread pinkly out from
cloud cuticles endlessly zigzagged peaks.

SKID MARKS

I thought I's movin' fast and gettin' stronger
I thought the coast was clear
Till I look'd in the mirror
And saw a set of skid marks gettin' longer
—Butch Hancock

His second wife was married her first time
in a Minolta-worthy English priory
beside a cemetery beside the sea.
Near the stone font on the west porch
where the newly wedded pass through crypt
and effigy and enter daily life,
a Pietà, larger-than-life, cradles the drowned
Shelley in her marble arms. *Which stands for what,*
exactly—poets doomed like marriage vows?
is what he almost thought to cry out, standing
with her there in front of all this
on his first visit to her past. That time
he managed to think twice, for once, before
he spoke. (Brought from Livorno by his wife,
the poet's heart, declared a sign beside
the statue, now is housed in the cathedral
some miles away.) And now he's thought so long
about it, his own home's grown calm. The kids?
Not yet asleep, but calm. His calm has rocks.
He counts out two, and pours. He knows how she
has counted out the nights he's lain beside
her, funerary both, each looking up,
perhaps a bit fed up, or else, unless
it's just *his* wish—he, like the kid he kids
himself he still is; she, his "Passionata,"
that figure in the medieval fresco *not*
the painter's real wife—they both are counting
still on nights when they will find a way

to tongue each other's voice, leaving for dead
Elsewhere's sculpted dead, so that together
they speak everything that cannot be said.

CONFUSION'S CURE

Confusion's cure lies not in such confusion.
—Friar Laurence in *Romeo and Juliet*

When the water's too low
you can't hear the church bells

when you're down on your knees
you're already up to your neck

can you hear the cell phone ringing

when constellations of geese
are fellating the starstruck skies

and you can't stand any longer
the long moonlit moraines

of near-misses

because the days of roadside
asparagus have been poisoned forever

and all that's left
is line static

load curve and loss margin

because the bedroom's become a Congressional
hearing issuing blanket-subpoenas

and the hydrogen economy
seems the only solution

—that or more disposable income

it's then you remember how you can't forget
how you blame me and accuse yourself

indemnifying our double
identities against their failure

to be identical

which is why you get so angry
declaring you can't wait

till death do us part
which is why tears are needed

washing away the detritus of desiderata

which is why the two of us seem
like the three Sunday boats out of here

first boat last boat late boat
me offering under you only

these buoying hands

HANG UP PLEASE AND TRY DIALING AGAIN

A baby is crying at the top of the house
all the while a story is forming
at the foot of the stairs. The one
painting in the room to the right
of the stairs is keeping watch above the baby
grand, which keeps its shape squarely
in the corner. No light is changing
now so as to alter any instrument,
much less the black lines stacked
with notes like waterspouts falling
off the edge of the page, much like
a paraphrase of motion or like the shape, even,
of the mind itself. Yours, say, more than
mine. Now, there are no longer any
reflections—or light, for that matter—
in the windows. And how could there be
with bottle after bottle rolling downstairs,
each one just missing the chocolate Lab
who is asleep by inches? That ringing—
is it the telephone or the sound of falling
into one of our other voices, blue
and dying, like babies in their mothers'
leafy arms? How cold it has been
all summer—every evening, almost,
calling for a fire after the after-dinner
brandy and the small talk about what
stopped being worth even the time of day.

POUSSE-CAFÉ

i.

Peering into her cell phone like a mirror,
Liliana is all like: "maybe I'll just
call the butcher"—because she is, in fact,
in the act of thinking. She is thinking:
tomorrow night luau, osso buco the next—
for she is Liliana, planner of celebrated
events, some of which require boutonnieres.
Organic always, her cuisine is also
multicultural, its hybridity
veering towards "fusion" but avoiding that oh-
so-dated waltz into the heterodox.
Casual slacks like khakis are *verboten*;
invitations *de rigueur*, like menus.

ii.

If celerity is celebrity.
then to look at Liliana
is to see why—who has
a head of hair a lover
could fashion a walled
medieval city out of,
a waist of dark chocolate
swathed in cheesecloth,
hips like flapjacks
on January Montana
mornings, breasts recalling
a Pope's favorite dessert,
neck like Béarnaise, a way

of standing, of waiting for you,
as a roux does, going amber,
a way of facing you, lips
apart, as one who forks
the lady-fingers from a trifle.

iii.

Will you pick up, Liliana, if I ring you?
I want you to arrange for me a glamour
so clocked into the grammar of
what's substantial that Taste may find
its one true sommelier, Beauty,
and celebrity become a thing to celebrate—
the way it happens all the time, we're told,
in Norway when they bring to the sauna
a skid of books, not to stoke the fire (for
there's a cord of hardwood waiting) but
because everyone is so certain there will be,
afterwards, after the dry heat and after
the freezing plunge, all the time in the world.

*(Pousse-café is a rainbow-striped after-dinner
drink made by floating up to 7 liqueurs into a tall,
thin glass according to the specific gravity of each.
Drinking it with a silver straw is traditional.)*

A PROBLEM, EXPLAINING

Sometimes when I finish a painting—
I mean, of course, not whenever I just
finish painting but when I finish finally,
really finish, painting *a* painting,
although I'm no longer actually sure
I know exactly when I've done so,
I feel like I could kiss myself.
And then the next moment I'm thinking
maybe this is not what I ought to be thinking,
which is what leads me to think I should be
feeling like, if I *were* to kiss myself, I would
want it to be the way I would want to be
kissing my wife, those times when she is
really happy that I am wanting to be kissing
her. Which is always a bit of a problem,
isn't it—explaining? Sometimes she even tries
painting that scene herself, that happy scene
of herself wanting me wanting to kiss her
more than I might be wanting to keep on
painting that painting which would begin
to explain why I may not be able as yet
to stop mixing my utterly unheard-of
colors up, why I can't stop myself long enough
to listen to her trying to explain how I could
learn from her how to finish whatever
it is I am still painting, which, as she would
likely remind me, I am doing, aren't I,
really for her, in the first place, after all.

ABOUT BANANAS

They would risk
the fire and the earth
and the water
and all
just to eat
a sack of bananas.

—Faulkner, *As I Lay Dying*

The fruit is blind.
Only the tree sees.

—René Char

1)

From an underground root-stock
an apparent stem rises.

Fully arisen, its closely
enveloped leaf-sheaths

and corresponding blades
form a spreading crown.

A true stem develops
at the flowering period

and bears fruit—
these erect, dense clusters.

2)

That's the thing about bananas:

even the word does not stay straight.
(To know how to spell it

is to know when to stop.)
Recumbent in a glazed bowl

they nod to one another
like estranged Quakers

shooting the noon breeze
with a pair of Panamanians

stripped of the energy
required daily.

Apples ripen beside them,
glowing like lamps

when no one speaks.
A handful of full-blown

peaches nestles among them,
skins tightening

at the first sign of dark.

3)

Peel back whatever husk you can.
Salvage the good as it comes.

Slit lengthwise with a damp knife.
Dust with brown sugar.

Fry, adding cognac.
Before it's too late, touch

carefully any flame to it.
Like the smudging of orange groves,

a blue light will spread
over the stacked plates,

the stripped carcasses,
down the hall-stairs and through

each loop of the chandeliers,
the ranks of demitasse arrayed.

Center what you have
in a warm place

where it can be
shared by everyone.

4)

Standing under yet another
bargain-basement still-life
signed in block print
like a ransom note,

a rare beauty replies,
"My mother made me eat
everything." To the right of center,
a solitary fruit is being fingered.

It is two feet long and thick
as a man's arm (an adequate
meal for how many
one hesitates to guess).

Quick licks across the lip
insinuate a mustache.
The tip of a dull knife
starts peeling the wrong end,

perpendicular to the ear
of a Panamanian man.
For as long as it takes,
two women, one in,

one in front of,
the painting, go on
arranging themselves
eccentrically like guitars.

5)

That's what I mean about bananas:
the duplicitous facts,
the ubiquitous stories!

An unripe fruit
is rich in starch
which, in ripening,
changes to sugar.

Hence, the undue
abdominal development
of those who live
mainly on this article.

(This is a fact.
It can be tested.
It can be proved
or disproved.
Lived with.)

6)

The hostess pivots on her spiked heel.
Ice clicks in the champagne creel.

A glass slides, stem first,
toward the tray's edge
like a door latch.

In the cocktail dark
a couple pauses;
they notice the parlor,
the tender-headed flowers.

Milling about the half-drawn curtains,
the sun slopes up the parquet
and deltas in the epergne.

Someone bends over
to spear the diced fruit
from a chilled cup.

The bar hums softly
like a Brussels sprout.

Cupping his own elbow,
a man in uniform
eyes a well-dressed woman
in the full-length mirror
just as she comes to the end
of her speculations on the divan,
a crisp, faintly yellow
antimacassar haloing
her tight curls.

Snack plates stop passing in mid-sentence.

I find myself catching my breath
beside you, under the taut fronds,
the straw-tinged, octopus-winged
unfolding green.

7)

Rolling one back like an eyelid,
do you find yourself rooted
in spite of yourself?

Does your tongue
loll in its place, rounded
with its little crown of dark?

Does your mouth work
in circles of anticipation
like a fish?

And are your fingers curled?
Do your feet slip
all over the place

even if you know nothing of Stonehenge,
even if you have never visited Panama
or recalled one childish threat that was serious?

Are you like someone, some hombre or chappy,
eating alone the breakfast of fruit
and crunchy granola his honey has left him,

in lieu of an explanation
for having gone about, without him,
her difficult development

for good?
That's just it.
I am.

8)

All right, then.
Now you know the facts.

Are we friends?
Shall we call it an end?

At some point doesn't it
just come down to trust?

My mind is weary
and the bed is hard.

Good night.
Sleep tight.

9)

And so I find myself
lolling here still beside you.

"Trust?" you whisper
from where you lie on your

side, "I have my own stories,
too. What about them?"

O fluent connoisseur!
I know you! You can use

a word like "appertain"
and really mean it.

And you? How can you
doubt the indelibility

of second chances? You hold them
out like a hand, a match,

there at the edge of the landscape
where moonlight

dripping from your gown
pools into small birds

at your feet, where
trees cross their arms

like chaperones ready to
shut this party down

outlet by outlet.
Words, you see, words—

the likes of you,
the likes of me:

here they come,
each of us, all of them,

bending to the touch,
closer now than my voice,

keeping the distance
between us.

We are sitting halfway
up in bed, as if reading.

Shadows raise the figure-8
of your breasts to the next

power, the droll
hypotenuse of my cock

countering the dark's
right angle. Look,

I can't even
keep a straight face.

Listen, I don't have to
tell you this.

INTIMACIES:
A Chorale

Poets though divine are men
—Ben Jonson

Poets are not celibate divines
—W. H. Auden

Sometimes of course I surprise myself
Playing the role of an incandescent lover
(Because I am not a wooden saint)
But that is not the way I think of myself
—Nicanor Parra
trans. Miller Williams

1. STUDY FOR THE FIGURE OF TIME

So fine those hips   the muslin sheathed
the sheathing showed   how movement moved
like a fingering of flutes   seen before the sound
warm as breath   can be blown through
      time's cold hands

2. EMBOUCHURE

And that is why, the next time,
before the morning light broke
and he woke to find her wanting,
he said it, tensed under all those
loosening folds that cannot wait
the uncovering of any coming light.
I can't lie here all day was what
he thought he heard her answer
pressing forward in his left hand
her forgiveness. Had there been,
from the beginning, any other
way to say it—when the light, say,
broke on them first in waves,
then rustled back across the floor
like sand? To be pleased was not
her pleasure? He almost thought it,

let it drop. And so
here they are together, these two.
He offers her a drink, he stokes
the fire. She, caring less for the drink
than the fire, he, caring less for the fire
than for another story, finger together
in their hands of glass the pages
of another dénouement where nothing
was left out. That's what he wonders
also, tapping ash: how all of this
holding on was touched off. They reach
outside the fire's light, his hand
on her hip, her finger drying his lip,
the night turning aquamarine,
which will by morning solidify
again as water, water.

3. CABBAGE HAULING

The rumble of cabbage trucks at dawn
bobbing to the wobble of shot U-
joints, loose axle-rods, the side planks
slapping against flat beds, hydras
of stammering cabbage heads
whitened with lickspittle hoarfrost,
knotting like water at the brim ...

The rumble of cabbage trucks at dawn
is shaking each window's white crosses,
the fractals of frost etched in each pane,
because even a tap coming on can shudder
houses as old as these. In one room
a cloth corners an eyelash, in another
a foot juts from under patchworks of quilt.

Then all at once the whole load shifts.

The rumble of cabbage trucks at dawn
is rolling coffee steam off a Styrofoam rim
wedged between glass and dash. Smoking
at the wheel, with a sweep of his sleeve he clears
the road ahead, punching in 90.3 with his thumb,
dreaming all the women he will never sleep with
and the nights that turned into awls and rasps
and the dawns he just keeps hauling past.

4.

When the gods make love
they are said to prefer
the woman above

the way her hair falls
open like a fan

the way her eyelids
tremble like her thighs

from the Prakrit,
after David Ray

5. ALBA

It's not yet day,
       Sweetness.
The lark lies.
       Light's not
What's meant.

from the Provençal

6. ASKING FOR IT

OK—to start,
we've got each other,
right? You, right there,
poring, tea-stained,
over star-charts,
predicting if this
winter storm will last
or whether it will be
the last, and me, just
here, still counting on
a sudden April flurry
more than on you.
Patience: it means
to suffer. *Que sera
sera*. We're not the
the sort to mope about
pour passer le temps.
So, toss those tea leaves,
honey, on the fire,
and tell me once more
what it was you were
about to (here,
sit on this) ask. ...

after Horace, Odes 1.11

7. YOUR FEET

When I cannot look at your face
I turn instead to your feet.

Feet of arched bone,
your hard little feet.

They support you, I know,
the sweet weight of you
that levitates on them.

Your waist and your breasts,
the concentric purples
of your nipples,
the hollows of your eyes
when they've just taken flight,
your wide fruit mouth
and red curls,
my little tower,

I adore.
But not your feet

except when they walked
up and down on the earth
and on the wind and even
on water
just to find me.

after Pablo Neruda

8. HER PRAYER

Now I lay me down
      you are the one
I want to press between
      these circummortal
hemispheres of me,
      my space, where I
make space for you,
      a vale the poet called
his Julia's *via lactea*,
      & as I pray to
wake, I make this
      morning wish anew: to place
you so, so that
      by pressing both of mine
around the whole
      of you, with both my hands
I move you up
      & in & down
& through
      & by extending you
renewing us, until I
      cry for you to
bless me with 'white love'
      that only you bestow
across my lip
      & on my chin
& in my tawny hair

after Archilochus & Robert Herrick

9.

Here is how
it is written

> **She openeth her mouth
> with wisdom and on her tongue
> is the law of kindness**

> *So how will you
> make me come?*

Here is how
it is written

> **There be three things
> which are too wonderful for me—
> yea, a fourth I cannot fathom**

> **the way of an eagle in the air
> the way of a serpent on a rock
> the way of a ship in the ocean's middle**

> **and the way of a man with a woman**

> *I will tell you, honey,
> when it's only a toy
> and not a plaything*

Here is how
it is written

> **The adventure that is
> a man and a woman
> requires so many
> feats of intimacy**

What you got
going there,
Hot Stuff?
A poem?

Here is how
it is written

At sixty now, or over,
Boss-Lady of Desire
Am I too softened
For your hard vows … ?

10.

Her heels off the floor
weight forward
one hand
holding his hip
for balance
the other
otherwise
occupied

11. HIS COMPLAINT

When even candlelight begins
to show how very old you've grown,
spooling and spinning by the fire,
you might be mouthing to yourself

some line I wrote once, then look up,
a bit surprised, and murmur, "Oh
that Ronsard—how he praised me so
back then"—when, starting at my name,

your girl will wake up, with a blessing on
your own. And me? I'll be long dead, one
of the myrtles' boneless ghosts.

And you? Almost so.

        The roses of life!
Pluck them all, quick, now, at once—
there in the dimness where you work
regretting love, your fierce disdain, my art. ...

after Pierre de Ronsard

12. STEERING BY SIRENS

Pockets of rock hollowed by water
emptied singing
this is the driftwood of women
who cannot be
said to be beauties

Their eyes assume the whiteness
of terns crying
across salt flats
how salt extracts what is delicate
from limbs awash in abalone and coral

Wrapped to the staff of your vessel
the ineluctable tide-lick
your prow thrusting to it
the chain-link
mail of the sea

for once all you need do is listen
relinquish your craft to the fallible
stout hands of others
here seamen
there houris
and for once in your life just listen

roiling in suffering's unspeakable joys

13. SCIENCE FICTION

all planets emit light
and indeed all bodies do
—Zukofsky, "A"-10

Plait by plait, his fingers
begin undoing
each of her braids,

the body of her
hair coming to
just below her shoulders,

and then the quick
undoing of all
that remains of her

apparel, and of his,
so that both their bodies
waver now in every wave

of air, like migratory
static, snow, the wake
toggle switches make

in their arc between
up and down,
leaving off for on.

No sun or planet
anywhere, everywhere
she touches him

he touches her,
their radio voices
cadenza-ing,

obbligatos rising
from the to and froing
in the strings.

As their bodies light
crackling with snatches
of melody, space

unfolds again
into the stillness
what comes and goes.

Hold this please he says
and there she is—herself
and every finger he has

taken from her face.

14. "AND TALKS TO HIS OWN SELF, HOWE'ER HE PLEASE"

Night had fallen
out of the blue
the moon beamed
among the lesser stars

twining all over him
like ivy up an oak
she swore this oath
repeating after him

I will love you
        until the last wolf
                drops dead in his tracks
until Orion stops
        jinxing our seamen
                as long as the hair
of Apollo
        uncurls
                in the wind

And so?

Haed ye one shard o manhood
left in ye
ye'd nae mair put up wi'

watchin her
nicht after nicht

taakin it in
givin it oot

to aa cumers
an' stop
talkin to yairsel

Aye, laddie,
that ye wud

And now who's this
strutting below in the leaves

rich and handsome
with land to burn

Listen, you—
the mysteries of Pythagoras:
learn them

this woman
one day will leave you
and when you're standing here

"amazëd like a sot"
don't look for me
to be laughing my ass off

like this
believe me

after Horace, Epode 15

*(The title is from "Caliban Upon
Setebos" by Robert Browning.)*

15. LAYING THE TABLE

The Table is not laid without
Till it is laid within.

—Emily Dickinson

If I wanted to make you love me
I would make you seafood, Honey,
not pasta, bisque perhaps or chowder,
and I'd serve it to you in the thickest,
reddest, heaviest, fine-figured
terracotta plate I could find

for Apulians like you and I
know cuttlefish from squid
from octopus, a periwinkle
from a cockle, flounder from sole
or plaice, scallops from sand-dollars

—a plate, I mean, with a crater, a little
omphalos or enticing concavity
in the middle of it, inscribed
with signs that say *dip things here.*

But that was all before Darius, who worked it out
       long before I met you;
Darius, who isn't "into" pasta, who can't tell bucatini
       from angel hair from al dente;
Darius, who is Greek and gay and has, I think you know,
       his eye on you.

(On a red-figure Apulian plate, 4th c.
BCE, attributed to the Darius painter.)

16.

I was kneeling
sideways
on a chair
and took him
in my mouth
and him
in one hand
and him ...

and you
at the same time
from behind

It was a kind
of dare,
the chair
and all.

(Sing hymns
they say
at heaven's gate.)

17.

They come to your window less & less often,
boys plying your shutters with pebbles,
robbing what's left of your beauty
          of sleep.

It might as well be a fist, the way your door
jams in its frame, so unlike the way
it used to bang open every time anyone
          came crying

out loud in the night how hard he got
wanting you, Sunshine. So, what we have
here are signs. Your turn has come. Alone
          you will roam

moonless back alleys, while the north wind
licks life into dead embers, lifts the haunches
of mares for the thrusts of their stallions
          to warm them . ...

for now is the time when everyone's grown
younger than you, seeding their loves
in groves where the leaves never yellow or blow
          off in the wind.

after Horace, Odes *1.25*

52

18. CARNAL SUITE

i.

She's bolt upright on my eyelids
        her hair in mine
She takes the shape my hands have made
        the color of my eyes
She's engulfed by my shadow
        as a stone by the sky

        Always her eyes
are open they never let me sleep
        By noon her dreams
have made whole galaxies evaporate
        & me I'm laughing
crying & laughing speaking without

        a thing to say

ii.

For having pictured everything I wanted
Your lips set in the sky of your words like a star
For kissing the night alive
And the wake of your arms down all sides of me
Forming a flame to stand for triumph
My dreams my love
Remained within this world
Transparent and without end.

And when you are not here
I dream I'm asleep dreaming I'm dreaming.

iii.

Sleep took a print of your body
And the color of your eyes

iv.

Their shoulders held high
In a way that says "attitude"
They look such looks these
Women in love that you
Lose your place trusting
What descends from the steep
Dawn of their breasts with rosy fingers
To undress the night

Eyes to crush stone
Smiles that don't give a damn
For any dream
Flurries of snow-cries
Lakes of nakedness
And shadows all uprooted.

All they leave one to believe in
Are glances, words, and kisses,
And to kiss their kisses only

Here I am showing only your face
The thunderheads of your throat
All that I know and all I'm unaware of
My love your love your love your love.

after Paul Eluard

19.

The beauty
of illusion

is that
its beauty

remains so
only for

as long
as it

stays illusory—
as now,

when she
bows, kneeling

before him,
her head

uplifted so
he may,

if he
wishes, think

this is
a kind

of worship,
worship of

him, and
not just

a way
of easing

his entry
into her

while exciting
her fear

that what
she wants

and he
prayed long

for was
after all

the beauty
of illusion.

20. WHAT SHE THINKS NOW
WHEN SHE THINKS OF IT

And now, nearly past
    the middle of her
life, did she ever
    like it, really?
Didn't she wish it
    more like opening
a bag of chips and
    less like finishing
them? All of it went
    too fast, took place too
often, tasted much
    too much like salt. From
the time when cooking
    was for her a way
of wooing, she would
    remember Julia
Child saying, "Fritos?
    They're cheap, addictive,
and I can't make them
    myself." She does not
remember Robert
    Frost's remark about
how his daughter couldn't
    make a whore house.
And yet it's sex, or
    something nearly like,
that she is thinking
    about near the time
she wants to answer
    the only question
she ever tries to
    ask any longer:

"So, what did I make?"
    —a pretty spicy stroganoff
    —a beautiful daughter
    —a generally happy man

21. CORONA

Out of my hand fall eats its own leaf: we're friends.
We shell time from the nuts and teach it to walk:
time returns to the shell.

In the mirror it's Sunday,
in dreams there's sleep,
mouth says what's true.

My eye moves toward my beloved's sex:
we exchange looks,
we say dark things,
we love each other as poppy and memory,
we sleep like the wine inside mussel shells,
like the sea in the blood-beam of the moon.

Standing at the window now we embrace, the people
          look up from the street:
it is time they knew!
It is time that the stones deigned to bloom,
that unrest got a heart-beat of its own.
Time now that it were time.

It's time.

after Paul Celan

22. LUST, AT YOUR AGE

A cello with no
need so dire
it stirs any echo

A viola with a
lilt so tender it
fills every hollow

A violin as un-
equivocally civil
as a stand

of sugar maples
that first warm week
before they run

23. OLD SUITS

The double-breasted
one was olive,
soft to the hand
as anything he
ever held her in

(He never held her
in.) Was it out-
grown, then? Or worn
out? Did Goodwill
get it, post-nup?

Another was charcoal,
a creamy ash
with fine pink
stripes and outward
facing pleats.

You can't fold suits
away like shirts.
They hang naked
in closets, racked
like cards,

a house of cards.
Irony, she knew,
was not enough
to leave him with.
So, she played

her hand out—
club, spade, diamond,
heart. But the diamond
it was cut deepest,
not needing flesh.

24. CONVERSATION, WITH FEELING

They sat together in the park
As the evening sky grew dark ...
They walked along by the old canal
A little confused, I remember well.
　　　—Bob Dylan, *"A Simple Twist of Fate"*

In an old city park, remote and iced over,
A moment ago two figures passed through.

Their eyes were glazed and their lips were gray.
It was hard to hear what they had to say.

In an old city park, remote and iced over,
Two specters, spelling out how much to renew.

—The trill of it all! Has it stayed with you?
—Why? Why wish that memory on me?

—So, your heart doesn't skip at my name?
No trace of me's left in your dreams?　—No.

—Who timed how long we kissed?　Who needed
Words for what we had to say?　—So you say.

—How blue the skies were! The future beaconed afar!
—The future? Beaconed? That lightless star?

Along they strolled among the stricken grasses,
Their voices lost on all but the darkness.

after Paul Verlaine

25.

The next night
and for many nights to come
he learned about dancing
and the head of a pin

the press of her breasts
together pressing
himself between

or one leg
lifted slightly
on an arm
of the chair

the full press of him behind

rocking her
rocking chair

26.

Sprinkles fell
afterwards
on his solitary
drive home
beading the wax
like age spots

27. NOCTURNE IN F MINOR

At first so
pianissimo

it seemed
less a way

of talking
than a place

to place
their hands

what she called
"making time"

(or was it
"taking time")

but that was
"then"

before any
"before"

was found
for them

to turn back to
or turn into

their own way
of "keeping time"

thanks to their
accelerando of hands

their tremolos
of surfeit

their pizzicati
of friction

their needy way
of knowing

how to keep
from knowing

how hands fall away
casual as breakage

Hast thou known
a nest softer

ran their fingers
down the keys

or
a harder end?

28. SISTER NOIRE

for Sister Anne-Marie

There is a certain danger coming
back to it like this after so long
the cabin in the woods filled
with women emerging each morning
without their habits most of them
without even their veils making
their way among us so few could tell
who was in service to which vow
or what it looked like in practice

this one my favorite

whose long red hair came to an end
in easy curls whose easy laugh
took all derision out of laughter
no piece of jewelry whatever
just one small cross no bigger
than a button on a vermilion
chain so slight I only saw it
fast on her flushed throat
when we stopped dancing

29. YOUR VOICE

Under this blowing blue-paned spring raincoat
I've nothing on, your voice is gentle
unbuttoning me, kissing me first on the shoulder

your name buttons my lips
closure sweet as abandon

my blue-paned spring raincoat swings
off me so naked your voice embracing
my waist as we run and we run but can't make it
                    even as far as the river

                    after Zeynep Uzunbay

30.

My love, if I should die and you do not,
or if you die, love, and I go on living,
we won't surrender any more land to grief:
the space we are inhabiting is room enough.

Dust from the wheat, sand off the desert,
weather, the moving water, a slack wind—
each transported us like winged seeds.
The moment to find ourselves could have passed.

As for the meadow where we now meet,
oh little infinity, we give it all back.
Because this love of ours, my love, is without

any ending: as it had no birth, so it knows
no death, it is merely long like a river
altering, as it passes, lands and lips.

after Pablo Neruda, "Sonnet 92"

31. DAPHNE: A PINDARIC ODE

I.1

And so the Pythian Games were created by Phoebus Apollo—
    a conversion of bloodlust into sport
which begat the victory odes sung by all the lords of the lyre,
    the Grecian mysteries and Italian dances,
and all because it took Phoebus, back then, his whole quiver
    to finish off Python, a monstrous beast
from the primal ooze, his mass vaster than empires and far slower.

I.2

On his way to the Games, his victorious locks hanging more thickly,
    more squarely, across his squared shoulders
than those of any three-ring impresario, any Siegfried or Roy,
    Phoebus mouthed off to the wingèd one,
he of the short and curlies, said to have his own quiver back home:
    So, what have you got in that quiver of yours
back home, big boy? Thus, Phoebus. The boy bit his tongue. Literally.

I.3

Later, atop Parnassus, his tongue still throbbing, the lad strung
    his little bow, and then nocked twin arrows,
one a (+), one a (-), a resistance completing the circuitry of desire.

II.1

The first one hits Daphne, her forehead bound in a tie-dye band,
    the kind a young *chanteuse* wears
in her early Folk-phase, hits her in the small of the back where

her fan of black hair, innocent of the rigors
of brushing, had stiffened. *Bad hair or no* her father cries *you're far*
    too beautiful to remain a virgin, but Daphne
is already laying out guitar licks for The Lady Di's, a girl-band.

II.2

At the same time, the other shaft hits Phoebus himself
    where it hurts the most, in mid-pursuit;
when it hurts the worst, he cries out to Daphne, though she is
    already under headphones, cries out through
little mouse lips of pain and passion and what passes in Phoebus
    for persuasion: *You mustn't leave*
all that dark wavy hair of yours forever unbraided, Beauty Fish.

II.3

Now he can't decide what to do next: hum (for nothing verbal
    is happening at his lips) or stop
and pout. Winded slightly, he stops. That's when he tries reason:

III.1

I'm not really all that bright, I know, but I have lands of my own,
    a mountain-top of powerful relations,
thousand-watt speakers, four of them, a fairly decent set
    of amps, designer drugs, a smile they'll write
lyrics of. And I love you. But she goes on fleeing, hummingbird-
    quick, gazelle-deft, hare-bent
on a hole to hide in, puce-red lava-flowers from a volcano erupting.

III.2

Turned hound-dog-mad now in pursuit of her streaming hair
        where it leaves on the furious wind heady
traces (he'll never forget what each of those words means), Apollo is
        flying faster than stags flee Apollo's arrows,
so fast he's become all god now, and he's at her shoulder, breathing
        into her hair, his moist breath finding
her ear, becoming her voice praying: *Change me, Father, change me.*

III.3

Apollo, spent, leans against her trunk. Her hair is cordage now,
        hanks of foliage. Her feet, roots. Her limbs,
limbs. *I swear I'll wear your leaves forever braided together with*
my hair. A wreath of yours will crown the head of every victor
        in sport and song. And like my own hair,
the leaves of the laurel will never whiten in the winter wind.

        Thus, Phoebus Apollo. As the wind went on throbbing,
the tree, locked in the throes of it, seemed almost to be nodding.

after Petah Coyne and Ovid

32. MOVIE DAY

————And then there's the one
about Lenny Bruce taking his son
to one of those grainy blue
movies they had back then,
taking him once the kid's matinee
was over, once the boy's Western
starring Lash LaRue was done.

   And just like that the boy
is asking   *What is that man*
doing with that pillow, bet he's
going to smother her, the way
he did it, the way it happened,
in the other one

   And Lenny? At first
he's daddy all over and just says

   Wait

   But this boy is a boy
who is not about to stop
being a boy about to stop
asking anything any time
soon   *So why is he putting it*
under her like that, that pillow,
it's a pillow, for pete's sake,
why is he doing that, is he
going to kill her now, sure
I bet he is, sure, look at
those hands …

And Lenny? He's more
Lenny now than father

Hey kid   shut up
OK?   just wait

And if the boy is dismayed
by any of this, it is only as one
who is about to discover
such things as peaches in the world,
clefts that soften, deepen
into hemispheres, and *look*
he's now saying *look he's*
kissing her all over the place
there   look   and there   and

even there

And Lenny? What he's doing
more of now is thinking
or what looks like thinking
or whatever it is we do

when our lips are moving
but nothing is there to be said
by us, no one is there

to speak for us

FURTHER
DISTURBANCES

TEXAS SLEEPING-CAR BALLADS

Just before pinking into flower,
the leaves of the oleander, a glossy
plant with arsenic in its leaves,
enough to kill a child, droop,
browning at the edges. Tropical
plants, even non-toxic ones—gardenias,
say, or aspidistra—are like this:
wanting them too much to flourish
one cuts them back too soon, at the first
suggestion of yellow, strangling the roots.
Better to let natural heat, mustering
what humidity it can, humor them
back to health. The fire-rot
across the pyracantha is something else:
this rust is systemic, probably fatal.
Of lavender and sage one shouldn't try
making Northern sense and water
in midsummer a dry root-bed.
Here is your garden—you, a modern
Eve among flowers but with other
places to be—and here is my life
at night, apart from you, reading about
botanical effects, screened against insects
matted against the light, dogs barking
up both sides of Loyola, F-16 Phantoms
downshifting the length of 290,
the sirens off Springdale outroaring
even the cicadas' outstretched wings.

*   *   *

Out of a nest buried
like a fossilized
pine cone in the bed
of a spider plant
hanging from the soffit

of the porch a pair
of fox sparrows
have mounted together
a trellis two feet from it.
These are not birds

that are slow to mate.
They hover and tread—
a little rufous fist
of feathers shaken
slashed at the wrist.

Why am I watching
long after my head hurts?

Chameleons
stop pumping
your pink throats!

*   *   *

Spring this year in Texas came
too warm, too wet, too soon.
These cottonwoods, their leaves
like hearts, have shed oh maybe
half, and still it is July and I
am here and raking leaves

half-heartedly and with the very
same raw throat and nose
I have to stop to blow
which I associate with shoveling
snow and raking other ovate
leaves October days when you
get wet, too warm, and soon
you're stripping layers, pushing
up your sleeves and itching
round your turtleneck--
soaking in the labor of it--
and shivering to the heart
too long after you stop.

*   *   *

Watch it, you said,
packing to go north:
a big rain now
will rot out the roots.

So I watch it
bruise and puff up
under clouds lobbed in
low like whiffle balls

someone stepped on
and broke.

*   *   *

Sure enough:

just like a child-proof plastic top—
one flick in the right place
only a child can master

and it's off.

*   *   *

To dry off I do figure-8's
around the rocking chair
and television set
ninety-eight, ninety-nine,
one hundred

and counting
my body slips when I walk
splitting every last seam
I'm a mango stinging
sweet with bat spit

thirty-six one-hundred-plus
degree days in a row
our ring road's exploded
birds are dropping
dead from the sky

which is what I'm getting at
when I try to sit still
I start counting
on you know what
for everything

*　*　*

Honey (I'm faxing
it to her) *how much*

*I miss you I know
you know* (words

to that effect).
It comes back

the old way,
wired, collect:

MORE THAN WHAT
TEND THE PLANTS
STOP

*　　*　　*

The male of the species holds the nape of his mate
lightly in his mouth: the base of his tail still bleeds.

Beneath her, the held earth is kneaded with claws.
For five seconds perhaps, three or four times an hour,

over several days, without sleep, in season—that's all it takes.
(Which of us counts, anyway, on a continuity of feasts?)

Slipping from him at last, in the blindness of daybreak,
stalking her own felled petals of light,

she stops once, perhaps, up ahead
to realign her next breath, caught now as scent,

and she becomes once again tameless,
a wild beast of mild desires—

hares, the odd gazelle, a strong limb in a tall tree,
high grass, shade. ... Though who knows

how to predict how any desire is tendered
across such complex distances,

hunkering among pampas grass or lying down
with wildebeest and moonshine?

Sort through a whole species' unkindnesses.
Perhaps you will find only one shard of real injustice

glittering in the long escarpment of resentment
but one will do, one will cement

the fossil record of suffering
and ensure the evolutionary tool be lifted

high upon a shoulder of righteousness
by someone childless who wants to drive it home.

THE PRINCIPLES OF ADULTERY

The first explains
how any ray (as of light)
passing between two points
will take the path that can be
traversed in the least time.

The second explains
how refraction occurs
when a wave (as of light)
passes between two different mediums
(such as water and glass).

1. *The Principle of Least Time*

Where they are standing   standing apart
hands together   a meadow comes to an end
in a handful of trees   collecting
what remains of the light   someone else
has passed through   night
and the creatures of night   gather
in the branches   of this room
a flush of fireflies   the print of bodies
in warm grass   he breathes into her
hutch of hair   long ago it is said
the forest closed   each of its doors
tonight   night may again
close its forest forever   at the flick
of a tongue   looks of adoration
and on high   the limbs of a sky
suddenly   full of birds
unfeathering   every bed

2. *The Sine Law of Refraction*

So the fox goes to ground
moths mat the screen the moon
rocks in its balls-heavy peace
which is the peace of those no longer
able to make their days consecutive
or to spend nights
those who wait and who wait
for when it will be nobody's fault
this way of acting not answerable
to anyone who doesn't add up
to someone particular enough
to stop that bouncing ball
the particulars of logic say
can never never stop
for there are those who did
matter once aren't there who didn't
mind perhaps at first or even
notice that they had stopped
counting though they don't stop
do they they never do because
of course there is no accounting
for it for desire for its parallaxes
its feelings that never learned
their place its tongues always failing
to keep watch its teeth leaving
traces all over the place
its map in the glove box with NOW
x'ed out and FROM HERE ON
OUT penciled in the repetition
of cell calls the roaming charges
the exquisite alarm at erring
in every direction at once driving
between states of ecstasy and a stoning

THE WOUND OF WATER IN
THE STONES OF THE DAY

At night I came to a stony town call'd Stone,
Where I knew none, nor was I known of none.

—John Taylor, "The Water Poet"

1.

Macadam

                whitewashed still

with winter's road salt

              draws a bead

between the barn and house

Beyond the barn

             below the house

the pond battens

           on outcrop

a pair of white monoliths

At the far end

            a failed dam wall

of charmed rock

             has gone under

intact

*

Down a clear line of sight
You can walk through
What's up country closes with
What you're passing between

*

Rosehips tumbled in tufts
                of ground ivy
Needles of fir softened underfoot

Ashes scattered out there
                across a cut meadow
Of stiff shocks surrounding a beech

Are those of a brother
                more my age than yours

2.

Beyond: mountains—
                the boundaries
of three states
                if you know

where to look
                a Moebius strip
of blue headlights
                if you don't

*

Once before I knew
anything and nothing

of course of you I met
a man named Moebius
who became a friend
an older friend as you
were first to me and who
wrote poems of his own

and didn't much like mine

Decades later our life
with each other over
you told me that decades
before we met he'd been
your brother's best friend
(it was Dickens, no, who
spoke of how common-
place coincidence is?)

*

Where the high road dipped
            you remembered
        ice collected most winters

such as the bad one
            when Thomas Wolfe came to visit
        and couldn't make it home

or the worse one
            when Frieda Lawrence lingered
        all afternoon in the library

admiring the stained glass
        and touched you once
     oddly on the head

which was long before
        what you knew
     included anything of me

3.

As a child you said   how you liked sledding
into that hollow   between the barn and house

hearing the strop   of runners on ice-pack
the hiss of salt   needling in

knowing by late spring   how still water
passes a fallen   stone wall over

(The title is a line from Yves Bonnefoy:
"La blessure de l'eau dans les pierres du jour.")

UPPER-AIR DRIVE-IN DISTURBANCES

My aim in painting
        has always been
                the most exact

transcription possible
        of my most intimate
                impressions of nature.

                —Edward Hopper

I was never able to
        paint what I
                set out to paint.

                —Edward Hopper

At noon a woman stands
        in a morning robe
                open in a doorway.

A woman and a bay
        window, herself
                in fuschia, the other,

a shade
        of lavender, she
                peers out from.

All in black
        in the loggia
                a blonde is thinking

maybe she'll choose
     a box seat. Intermission
         and she's never left

the front row.
     Elsewhere
         row upon row

of blank windows
     on an empty street.
         Like doggerel.

Like movie screens.
     Like strip
         malls.

Which reminds me.
     What does the sight
         of a woman disrobing

for bed mean
     to you? No,
         I mean you.

Or of a naked woman
     twelve storeys up
         in front of an open

window fighting off the way
     curtains wave at her breasts,
         purl against her chin?

Does it matter at what angle
        you see her?
                Are you dreaming

yet? Yes,
        I mean you.
                Bent knees, bottom

thrusting, sheets violet
        and chill between her
                crossed legs,

her breath wrinkled
        like a speaker hooked
                over a nearly

closed car window
        in a leveling
                wind barely audible.

FEMME PAYSAGE

From the trace of a vein
        on the left side
when you find her cheek flushed,
        to the further
bluing of it going
        down, then over,
like the way the sequence
        of a brush stroke
that forms a character
        that means desire
is drawn, like the way brown
        spots may now be
starring the flyway of
        the V that shapes
how her throat gathers dusk
        or where bird tracks
are vanishing under
        the curve of her
breasts, then running across
        the lily pads,
imprinting them also,
        on the now stilled
étang of her belly's
        landskip of bared
longing, at the smooth edge
        of which mallow
and sedge beard the burrow
        of what can just
be seen, so annular
        and submarine.

THE CONUNDRUM OF SUPPER CLUBS

We shall have everything we want
and there'll be no more dying
on the pretty plains or in the supper clubs.
—Frank O'Hara

What stays with me still, like the banjo
solo in a swing-era band, every time
I find myself thinking again of you
is what a "supper club" is, really. Which
is what you also wanted always to know,
not sure even then that you trusted my taste—
you with your uptown disapprobation
of drinks with grenadine or maraschino,
not to mention the doggy position,
not to mention your down-home view
of where you wanted both of us to be
this time next year (not to mention
after work tomorrow). So let me take you,
I would always like to say, whenever you
would play along, to one such club just
south of where I come from, just north
of the state line, on the fabled Highway
51 by the power plant beside the river,
near the old outdoor with two screens.
No, it's no piano bar. No members-only
rooms. No cover bands with banks
of mics deep-throating the saxophones.
A supper club was just my way
of picturing my old Rock-Island-Prairie
self to your svelte Pennsylvanian one,
leapfrogging yesteryear's bramble patch
with that rip in the seat of my pants
from trying to put a seal on every deal,
all the while trying to think—no, to dream

really (and amen to that)—of all the bee-
loud glades and pretty plains we might,
in spite of it all, end up at. All I wanted
back then was to see you more, to see
more of you, or just to see you through
this world of ringing things, text-
messaging one another—CANNED
MUSIC? LIVE?—to thwart the odds—
SPLIT CHEX? FULL BAR?—that we
would ever lay all our cards down—
CANT WAIT 2 C U LUV—on any
matching nightstands of deal.

CAREER MOVES

And if I ever lose my mouth
All my teeth north and south
                          —Cat Stevens

Don't capitulate to arithmetic.
                          —Barbara Ras

Of course I want to
do it exactly the way she
wants me to
because I like the way she is
when she is showing
me how to do it,
using her brush
to massage lightly without
abrasion, without making
any recession deeper.

So, here I am,
"of a certain age,"
trying to be
pleased with her
mouth-work, my
mouth, sharing secretly
that oh so American
fear of dentures,

when the B side of this 45
comes on at the corner
7-Eleven
every time I am handed a new
subset of the wrong change
for a Milky Way
by an adolescent in extremis—

and the particles of the "New
Math's" commutative disorders
left behind from the last quartile
of "America's Century"

find themselves wanting
to be flossed by the New Dentistry.

Bless you, Procter & Gamble,
for your decay-preventive dentifrice,
for mastering that whole Red-Scare-
fuelled fear-of-fluoride thing
but postmodern wisdom
prefers the prophylactic method:
extract third molars
before they even irrupt.

(In the hygienics of enamel
the cardinal issue
always reverts to ordinal value.)

Count for yourself, oh
ye who little can:
you get at most 32,
using base-10,
to fill the whole
pianoforte of your gums.

Never give up
any of them.

Back when I was still
sending my love,
she would write from Aruba
(herself a native Caraqueña,
therefore quite chatty) about her days
(they were short), about her nights
(grindingly long),
and then she would give me a piece of her mind,
bringing it home to me
how really incredible
she had been. That's when I tried
bringing it home to her,
banking on wired things
(flowers, say), then
sooner or later
poems.
Mine.
In feet she could count
on her fingers.
On overnight
contrails of Express Air.

The rest of my time I spent learning backgammon
or auditing colloquia at the local
university. My love?
Condensed matter –
myself, though, often as not
without the calculus to follow
that phenolic polymer interface.
(But I knew that,
didn't I?)
Or else I'd be out there
touring the continents with other big spenders,

getting it down, her out of mind,
getting to where I could be thinking
about that roller-coaster figure of a woman
and roll doubles every time.

And now?
Gingivitis-prone,
the wagging-the-tail-to-please part
of my maturity
turning, let's face it,
ugly –
what do I do?
Where can I go?
I smile, sure. Observe
in passing mirrors
how they're all there.
But what have I learned?
And is it commensurate with
what I've earned?
Whose fault is it,
anyway? Can you send out for anything
(pizza, perfume) to mollify
a lonesomeness like mine?

Commutative questions –
they're everywhere.
But me? I'm all,
as they say,
like elsewhere.

Days like these,
pulling off on the drive home, I want to
to put it down, add it up—exactly how much
love I've spent waiting
for it to catch on.

Nights like these,
I know what counts or what to count on
or at least how to keep
the poems that count inside
the barrier of my teeth.

AUTHOR'S NOTE

When I think about my blessings, and I often do, many individuals come to mind, so many that my short space here prevents me from constructing the endless monument I owe each of you.

I think equally gratefully of the institutions, academic or governmental, I do not need to thank for supporting my creative work, leaving me, in the words of the painter Fairfield Porter, "like an artisan who does his own good job for its sake ... and having no status to defend, may sing at his work, or make a dance out of it. ..."

An accomplished individual designer, Randolph Bertin, produced my first two books of poetry. The first, *The Halfway Tree*, a letterpress production on woven paper, prompted this remark from a poet-friend, "I don't have towels in my house as nice as that paper."

For the next book, *Black Butterflies*, Randolph's design incorporated the superb pinhole photography of Jesseca Ferguson in an intricate way involving both the book covers and the dust jacket.

I thank the late Palmer Hall, for his delicate editorial help and for publishing so many fine poets under the Pecan Grove imprint, including my volume *The Names They Found There*, one of his last. And thanks especially to Lance Letscher, who first gave me carte blanche to use any of his art on the cover of that book, and then, finding such visual tokenism inadequate, generously offered to design the whole cover. This largesse, and from a man I'd never met, embodies the finest illustration of art as gift-giving.

For help on the present book, and for his critical reading not only of what I have written but of contemporary poetry in general, I salute the astute Philip Pardi. Louisa Hall and Ken Fontenot: your timely remarks helped this volume reach this point. To Charles Rossman in Austin, John Burns in Galloway, and the Cunda International Workshop for Translators of Turkish Literature, especially Saliha Paker in Istanbul, thank you for crucial translation help. And Gary and Susan, curators of Pinyon Publishing: may the labors you've so beautifully begun prosper long and far.

The making of this volume was further blessed by the arrival of Ryker and Fleur and Arwyn. To Clare and Dane, Erica and Calum: you see how the fruits of your own intimacies go on to nurture the rest of us.

CPSIA information can be obtained at www.ICGtesting.com
Printed in the USA
BVOW02s1332160913

331259BV00001B/2/P